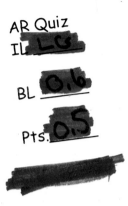

D1564710

Birds

by Helen Frost

Consulting Editor: Gail Saunders-Smith, Ph.D.

Consultant: Jennifer Zablotny, D.V.M.,
Member, American Animal Hospital Association

Pebble Books

an imprint of Capstone Press
Mankato, Minnesota

Pebble Books are published by Capstone Press
151 Good Counsel Drive, P.O. Box 669, Mankato, Minnesota 56002
http://www.capstone-press.com

2 3 4 5 6 7 06 05 04 03

Library of Congress Cataloging-in-Publication Data
Frost, Helen, 1949–
    Birds / by Helen Frost.
    p. cm.—(All about pets)
    Summary: Simple text and photographs present the features and care of birds
that can be kept as pets.
    ISBN 0-7368-0654-7 (hardcover)
    ISBN 0-7368-8782-2 (paperback)
    SF461.35 F.76 2001
    636.6'8—dc21   00-022976

Note to Parents and Teachers

The All About Pets series supports national science standards for
units on the diversity and unity of life. This book describes domesti-
cated birds and illustrates what they need from their owners. The
photographs support emergent readers in understanding the text.
The repetition of words and phrases helps emergent readers learn
new words. This book also introduces emergent readers to subject-
specific vocabulary words, which are defined in the Words to Know
section. Emergent readers may need assistance to read some words
and to use the Table of Contents, Words to Know, Read More,
Internet Sites, and Index/Word List sections of the book.

Table of Contents

Some birds can be pets.

Birds have wings.

8

Birds have feathers.

Birds have a bill.

Birds need food
and water.

Birds need a clean cage.

Birds need a place
to perch.

18

Birds need toys.

Birds need space to move.

Words to Know

bill—the hard part of a bird's mouth

cage—a container in which birds or other animals are kept; cages are made of wires or bars; birds need large cages so they can move.

feather—a light, fluffy part that covers a bird's body; bird feathers are many colors.

food—something that people, animals, and plants need to stay alive and grow; each kind of bird has a certain diet; birds eat mainly seeds, fruits, and vegetables.

perch—to sit or rest on a bar or branch; a pet bird needs a place to perch in its cage.

pet—a tame animal kept for company or pleasure; only certain kinds of birds can be kept as pets; wild birds are not good pets.

toy—an object to play with; pet birds need toys to keep them busy.

wing—one of the feather-covered limbs of a bird; birds move their wings to fly.

Read More

Hansen, Ann Larkin. *Birds.* Popular Pet Care. Minneapolis: Abdo & Daughters, 1997.

Heinrichs, Ann. *Birds.* Nature's Friends. Minneapolis: Compass Point Books, 2003.

Vrbova, Zuza. *Parakeets.* Junior Pet Care. Philadelphia: Chelsea House, 1998.

Internet Sites

Do you want to find out more about birds? Let FactHound, our fact-finding hound dog, do the research for you.

Here's how:

1) Visit *http://www.facthound.com*

2) Type in the **Book ID** number: **0736806547**

3) Click on **FETCH IT**.

FactHound will fetch Internet sites picked by our editors just for you!

Index/Word List

bill, 11
cage, 15
clean, 15
feathers, 9
food, 13
have, 7, 9, 11
move, 21
need, 13, 15, 17,
   19, 21

perch, 17
pets, 5
place, 17
some, 5
space, 21
toys, 19
water, 13
wings, 7

Word Count: 39
Early-Intervention Level: 5

Editorial Credits
Martha E. H. Rustad, editor; Linda Clavel, designer; Jodi Theisen and Katy Kudela,
   photo researchers; Crystal Graf, photo editor

Photo Credits
David F. Clobes, 1, 4
Jack Glisson, 12
Joan Balzarini, 6, 16, 18
Norvia Behling, 8, 10, 14
Photo Network/Tom McCarthy, 20
Photri-Microstock, cover

The author thanks the children's section staff at the Allen County Public Library in
Fort Wayne, Indiana, for research assistance. The author also thanks Nancy T.
Whitesell, D.V.M., at St. Joseph Animal Hospital in Fort Wayne, Indiana.